Jesus told a story to a big crowd by the seaside.

A farmer sowed seed in his field.

Some seed fell on the hard path. The birds ate it up.

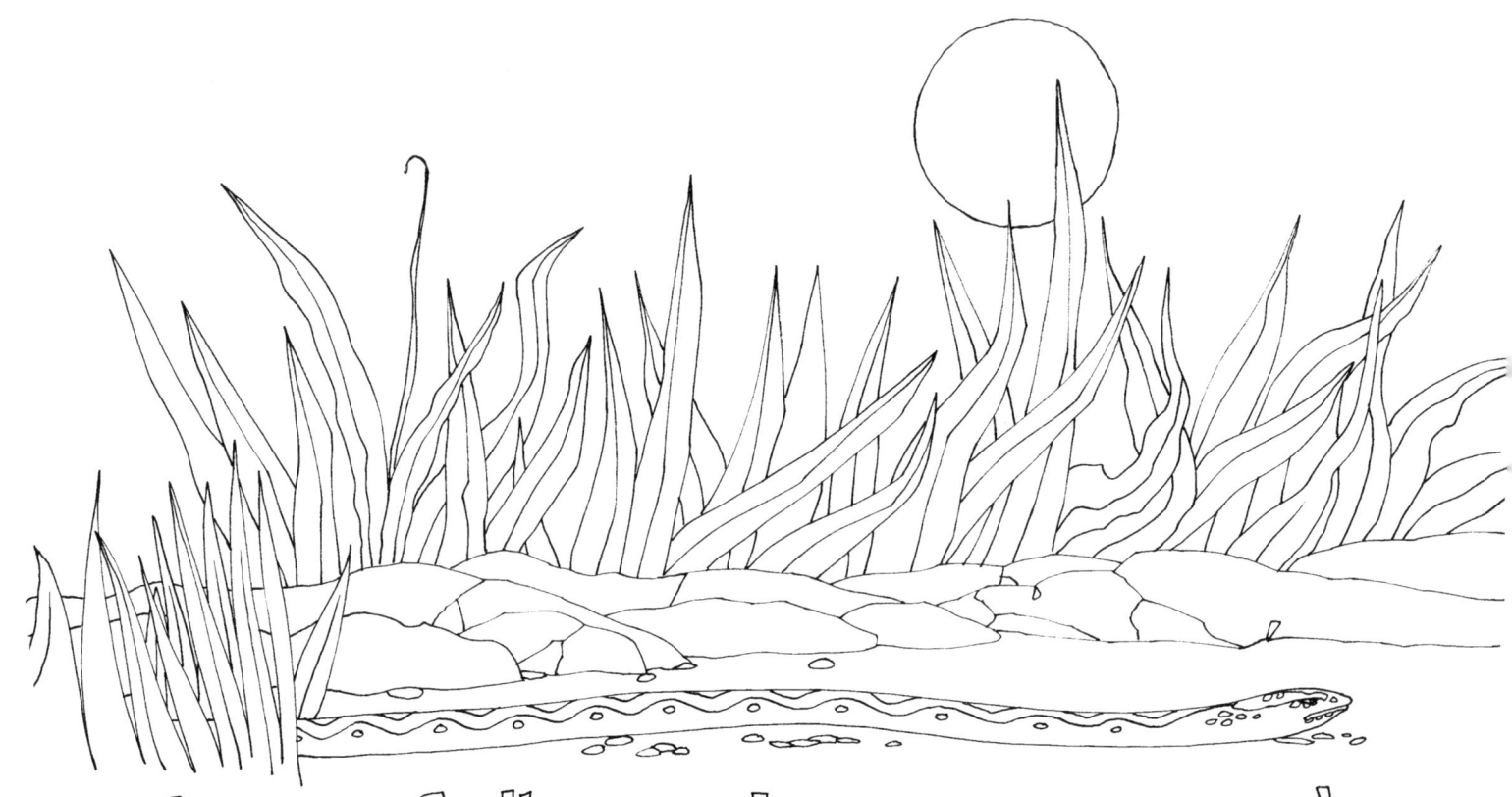

Some fell on stony ground.
The hot sun withered the plants.

Some seed fell among thorns, which choked the little seedlings.

But some seed fell on good ground. A good crop grew there.

Jesus told what the story meant.
The seed is the word of God.

Those who listen to the word preached are like different types of soil.

Some hear the word but Satan snatches it away and makes them forget.

Some hear the word gladly at first and seem to do well.

But when trouble comes they give up.

Others hear the word but soon other things take over.

Worries about money and getting lots of things choke the word.

Those like the good ground, hear the word and accept it.

It bears fruit in their lives like love, joy and peace.

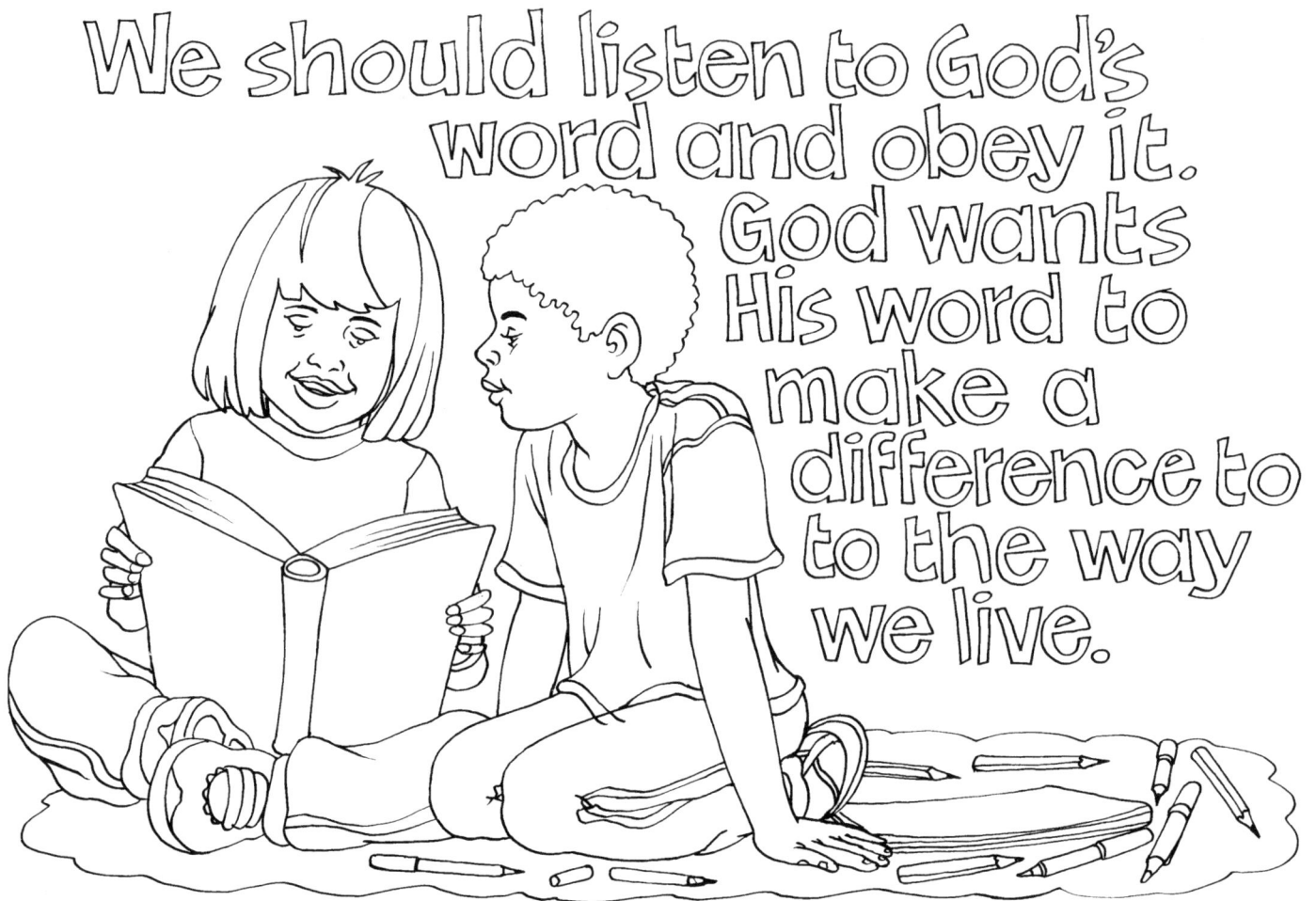